Discovery explore YOUR WORLD™

inside
PLANET
earth

By Steve Parker
Illustrated by Barry Croucher

Miles Kelly

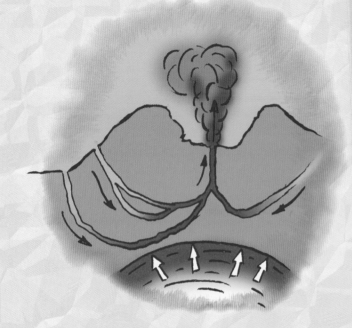

ACKNOWLEDGEMENTS

All panel artworks by Rocket Design

The publishers would like to thank the following sources for the use of their photographs:

Front cover: Science Photo Library: (c) Gary Hinks

Back cover: Shutterstock: (c) J. Helgason

iStock: 24 Rob Broek

NOAA: 32 Craig Smith, University of Hawaii; 35 Image courtesy of Submarine Ring of Fire 2006 Exploration, NOAA Vents Program

Photolibrary.com: 8 Fabrice Beauchêne; 10 Manfred Bail

Rex Features: 7(t) Aflo

Shutterstock: COVER Vulkanette, ostill; 6(t) gary yim, (b) Stephen Bonk, (c) Galyna Andrushko; 12 arindambanerjee; 14 Libor Pí ka; 16 J. Helgason; 18 Attila Jandi; 20 mountainpix; 22 ostill; 27 Liunian; 29 Masonjar; 30 Cloudia Newland; 36 Caitlin Mirra

All other photographs are from Miles Kelly Archives

WWW.FACTSFORPROJECTS.COM

Each top right-hand page directs you to the Internet to help you find out more. You can log on to **www.factsforprojects.com** to find free pictures, additional information, videos, fun activities and further web links. These are for your own personal use and should not be copied or distributed for any commercial or profit-related purpose.

If you do decide to use the Internet with your book, here's a list of what you'll need:
• A PC with Microsoft® Windows® XP or later versions, or a Macintosh with OS X or later, and 512Mb RAM

• A browser such as Microsoft® Internet Explorer 9, Firefox 4.X or Safari 5.X
• Connection to the Internet. Broadband connection recommended
• An account with an Internet Service Provider (ISP)
• A sound card for listening to sound files

Links won't work?
www.factsforprojects.com is regularly checked to make sure the links provide you with lots of information. Sometimes you may receive a message saying that a site is unavailable. If this happens, just try again later.

Stay safe!
When using the Internet, make sure you follow these guidelines:
• Ask a parent's or a guardian's permission before you log on.
• Never give out your personal details, such as your name, address or email.
• If a site asks you to log in or register by typing your name or email address, speak to your parent or guardian first.
• If you do receive an email from someone you don't know, tell an adult and do not reply to the message.
• Never arrange to meet anyone you have talked to on the Internet.

Miles Kelly Publishing is not responsible for the accuracy or suitability of the information on any website other than its own. We recommend that children are supervised while on the Internet and that they do not use Internet chat rooms.

www.mileskelly.net

info@mileskelly.net

CONTENTS

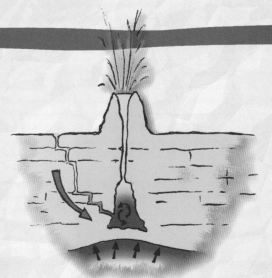

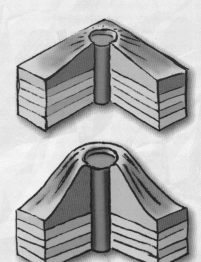

INTRODUCTION

Our planet is bigger than we can imagine. It would take more than a year to walk around it non-stop. Earth is also extremely powerful. Great events such as volcanic eruptions, earthquakes and tsunamis can easily destroy cities. From space, however, the latest satellite and spacecraft pictures show our the Earth as a small planet with water, land and clouds, hanging in the vast expanse of space.

Winds carrying sand scour 'wave rocks', shown here in Arizona, USA.

Air and water in the atmosphere move in a constant cycle.

Water vapour condenses to form clouds

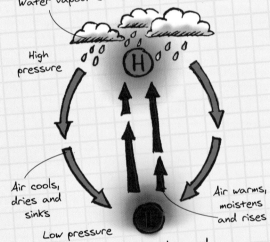

High pressure

Air cools, dries and sinks

Low pressure

Air warms, moistens and rises

Sun-warmed ground

OUTSIDE FORCE

Earth is rarely still. Wind, rain, falling rocks and running water never stop moving. One of the great driving forces for these changes is the Sun. Its heat warms some areas, such as dark soil, more than others, such as pale rocks. The warmth heats air and makes it lighter so it rises and sets up air currents or winds. The warmth also evaporates water into invisible vapour. This vapour rises too, then cools and condenses back into droplets, as clouds and rain. In this way the weather is always on the move, all around the world.

Since the continents first formed, some have travelled more than halfway around the globe.

The Himalayas are home to the highest peaks on Earth.

Sunset rays on high 'anvil' clouds create a spectacular scene

The topics in this book are Internet linked.
Visit www.factsforprojects.com to find out more.

FORCES WITHIN

Away from deep space and the Sun, there are gigantic forces deep within Earth itself. The centre of our planet has a temperature of 5500°C – almost as scorching as the Sun's surface – and the pressure is three million times more than we feel at the surface. These internal conditions work outwards to move huge sections of the planet's outer shell, called tectonic plates. This leads to massive global events such as earthquakes and volcanoes, as the continents drift and the oceans reshape around the planet.

Devastation followed the 2011 earthquake and tsunami in Japan.

UNDERSTANDING OUR PLANET

Earth sciences have advanced hugely in recent years. We know more about how glaciers slide downhill, how weather erodes rocks and how mountains rise from plains. But the vast scale of the Earth means we can do little to prevent great natural disasters. Even predicting a volcanic eruption or an earthquake is very complicated, with so many forces and factors at work. However more and faster early warnings should tell us when the planet is about to have one of its major 'shudders', and help to save thousands of lives.

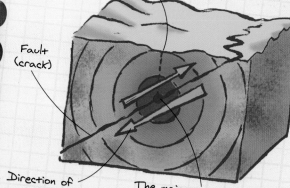

The place at the surface where an earthquake appears to occur is the epicentre

Fault (crack)

Direction of movement

The main movement is far below at the hypocentre or focus

INSIDE THE EARTH

The solid rock beneath our feet may seem like it has been there forever, but it is just a tiny part of the Earth's outer layer, or crust. In turn, the crust is a tiny part of the whole planet, making up less than 1/100th of its total volume. The bulk of the Earth consists of an immensely hot, enormously pressurized layer beneath, called the mantle. Within this is the even hotter, higher-pressure centre, or core.

Did you know?

The Earth's hard, rocky outer crust is thinner, in proportion to the whole planet, than the skin of an apple. In some places under the oceans, this crust is just 5 km thick. The continental crust (land) is up to 16 times thicker and so dips down deeper into the mantle.

The distinction between the outer core and inner core was not discovered until the 1930s. It was made using information from natural shock or seismic waves, earthquakes, and also artificial shock waves from explosions and other big vibrations.

✳ BORING boreholes

Holes are drilled into the Earth's crust for many reasons. We look for energy resources such as coal, oil and gas, also raw metals and minerals such as iron, aluminium and sodium in the form of rocky ores, and diamonds and other precious gems. We also drill boreholes for scientific research, to study how temperature, pressure and rock types change with depth. Rod-shaped cores of ice drilled from glaciers and ice sheets contain samples of air from thousands of years ago, giving clues to how past climates have changed.

Outer core This layer is about 2200 km thick. It is mainly iron with some nickel and is probably partly liquid, so that it can flow and generate magnetism (see opposite).

Inner core The centre of the planet is a ball 2400 km across made chiefly of iron, along with some nickel and other substances. It is so pressurized that it is probably solid.

Thin oceanic crust

Crust The rocky outermost layer is not a one-piece shell, but is broken into more than ten huge, curved, jagged-edged tectonic plates, as shown on later pages.

Ice core samples 3000 metres deep go back half a million years

Discover more about the Earth's interior with an interactive diagram by visiting www.factsforprojects.com and clicking on the web link.

Mantle About 2900 km deep, the mantle forms the bulk of the Earth. It consists of rocks rich in silicon, and also iron and magnesium. Its outer layers can just about flow, very very slowly.

The surface of the Earth spins once every 23 hours, 56 minutes and 5 seconds. But other parts inside spin at slightly different speeds.

Thick continental crust

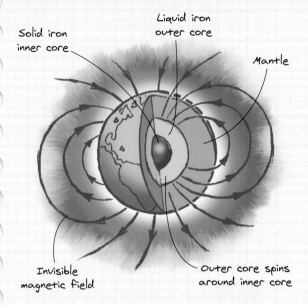

Solid iron inner core

Liquid iron outer core

Mantle

Invisible magnetic field

Outer core spins around inner core

✳ MEGA magnetic motor

The magnets we use in machines, such as electric motors, are made of iron-based metals. The core of the Earth is almost all iron, too. In the slightly liquid outer core, immense temperatures and pressures make parts of it flow very gradually with heat or convection currents, around the solid (but still spinning) inner core. This 'dynamo effect' is probably what generates the Earth's magnetic field. The magnetic forces are strongest along the line around which the core and the rest of the Earth spin – the planet's axis, which runs between the North and South Poles. The lines of magnetic force extend into space and fade with distance.

Atmosphere The layer of mixed gases we call air extends from the surface to about 100 km high, where it thins and fades into the emptiness of space.

Recent discoveries suggest the inner core spins faster than the rest of the planet, so it would make one turn more than the crust every 1000 years.

PLATE TECTONICS

The Earth seems so solid, still and unchanging – until there is a giant earthquake, a tsunami, or a massive volcanic eruption. These enormous events happen because the crust is actually quite thin and fragile, divided into several huge jigsaw-like pieces, called tectonic plates. The plates are on the move, easily pushed around by gigantic forces in the mantle beneath.

Did you know?

Each tectonic plate is composed of an area of crust plus a thin layer of the outermost mantle just below it. These crust-and-mantle pieces are an average 100 kilometres deep and form a shell-like layer, the lithosphere.

Laminar flow Different rock layers of one plate may slide at slightly different speeds and directions, for example, here causing the upper layers to buckle.

Rock is bent and squeezed up

The largest tectonic plate is the Pacific one with an area of 103 million sq km.

Crust layers The cutaway crust shown here is composed of layers of sedimentary rocks, formed originally from sand, mud and similar small particles. Other parts of the crust may be unlayered.

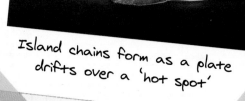

Island chains form as a plate drifts over a 'hot spot'

✳ SHIFTING islands

Here and there in the mantle is a geological 'hot spot', where its rocks are at an even greater temperature than the rest of the mantle. This molten rock (magma) pushes or occasionally bursts through the crust as a mantle plume, often volcanically in the ocean, forming an island. This may happen several times over millions of years to leave a chain of islands, each one younger than the next. Groups such as the Hawaiian and Galapagos islands probably formed in this way.

Subduction zone As a thin, light oceanic plate is forced against a thick, heavy, deep continental plate, it gets pushed down or subducted, and usually melts back into the mantle beneath.

A map of the tectonic plates is shown on page 19.

To watch a video showing how plate tectonics created the Earth's continents visit www.factsforprojects.com and click on the web link.

PANGAEA

North America
Eurasia
Africa
India
South America
Australia

200 million years ago: the supercontinent Pangaea was surrounded by a superocean

LAURASIA

GONDWANA

135 million years ago: Pangaea had split into northern and southern parts

✳ On the MOVE

Tectonic plates probably started moving some 4500 million years ago, soon after our planet took on its ball shape. Using evidence such as fossils, rock layers, and lines of magnetism 'frozen' into certain rocks as they formed, we can work out which plates have moved where. Some 200 million years ago, all continents were jammed together as one giant land mass called Pangaea. This slowly split into two, and continued to give the separate continents of today.

Volcano zone
Where the plate's edge is cracked and weakened by movement, liquid rock or magma can force through as a chain of volcanoes.

Mid-oceanic ridge zone The welling up of magma along a crack where two plates move apart forms a long ridge on the seabed.

The rate of oceanic plate movement has slowed in the last few million years.

Sea-floor spreading As magma solidifies along the diverging edges of oceanic plates, it adds to their size. This is known as sea-floor spreading.

The East Pacific Rise in the South Pacific is one of the fastest moving plate areas, at 15 cm each year.

Divergence zone
Two oceanic plates that move apart, or diverge, allow liquid magma to well up slowly from just a few kilometres below in the upper mantle.

The Galapagos micro-plate in the mid Pacific Ocean is just 1200 sq km in area, like a corner broken off its neighbour.

Most tectonic plates are moving in relation to each other by several centimetres per year — about the rate your fingernails grow.

EARTHQUAKES

Our planet's vast tectonic plates do not move past each other in a smooth, uniform way. Their jagged edges lock together and resist sliding as forces in the mantle build up and up, until suddenly the plates slip past each other and crack. The crust jerks and vibrates with colossal force. This is an earthquake. If it happens beneath the sea it may cause a giant wave or tsunami.

Did you know?

The magnitude or energy release of an earthquake can be measured on the Magnitude Scale. This is 'logarithmic to base 10', which means a quake of magnitude 5 has ten times the energy of one at 4, a magnitude 6 quake is ten times more energetic than one of 5, and so on.

The biggest earthquake ever recorded was near Valdivia, Chile, in May 1960. It had a magnitude of 9.5.

One earthquake can trigger another, resulting in several close together, called an earthquake storm.

Fault line On the Earth's surface, a fault line may show as a series of narrow cracks or a row of deeper canyons.

Transform fault This happens where two tectonic plates slide and grind sideways past each other, sticking for a time then suddenly slipping to produce a quake.

Meeting of plates

Whole cities can be destroyed by an earthquake

✳ TOTAL devastation

The amount of destruction caused by an earthquake depends on many features, not only its magnitude. These include whether the quake is near centres of human population, the types of rocks, whether there is a tsunami, and how buildings and structures cope with the shaking. In 1964 a huge quake of magnitude 9.2 in sparsely-inhabited Alaska resulted in 128 deaths. The Indian Ocean quake and tsunami of 2004, magnitude 9.1, killed more than 220,000.

Find photos, maps and more amazing facts about extreme quakes by visiting www.factsforprojects.com and clicking on the web link.

The Magnitude Scale for measuring great Earth movements has now replaced the old Richter Scale.

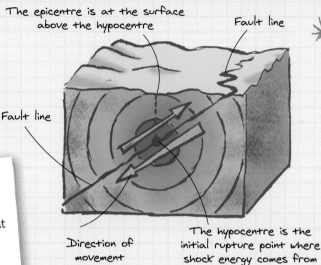

The epicentre is at the surface above the hypocentre

Fault line

Fault line

Direction of movement

The hypocentre is the initial rupture point where shock energy comes from

✳ Where's the FAULT?

Earthquakes release incredible amounts of energy as rock movements. The central place where the energy first emerges or radiates from, is termed the hypocentre or focus. This may be many kilometres under the surface. The shock or seismic waves spread out, up to the surface and sideways through the rocks, and also down deeper, as giant vibrations. The point on the surface directly above the hypocentre is known as the epicentre, and at ground level this appears to be the centre from which the waves spread.

Tsunami hits land
As the tsunami moves into shallow water, the pattern of its movement changes. It begins to rear up, like surf, becoming taller as it floods onto the shore and beyond.

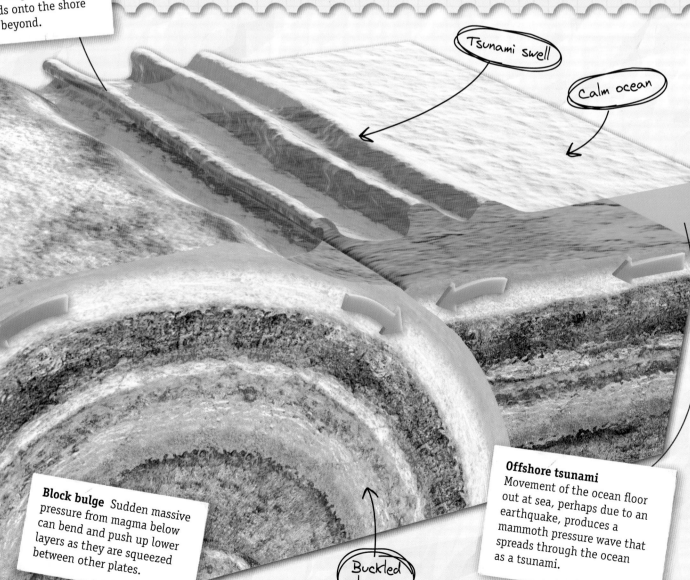

Tsunami swell

Calm ocean

Block bulge Sudden massive pressure from magma below can bend and push up lower layers as they are squeezed between other plates.

Buckled layers

Offshore tsunami
Movement of the ocean floor out at sea, perhaps due to an earthquake, produces a mammoth pressure wave that spreads through the ocean as a tsunami.

THE ROCK CYCLE

The basic ingredients of the rocks and minerals on Earth have been here since the planet formed over 4500 million years ago. But the types of rocks themselves have changed enormously during that immense time span. This is due to the rock cycle. Rocks are worn down or eroded by weather. They then collect in loose layers, harden into new rocks, become altered by great temperature and pressure deep underground, and even melt and then cool and go solid again.

Did you know?

Some of the oldest unaltered rocks are around Hudson Bay and in the Northwest Territories, both in northern Canada. They have been dated at probably more than 4000 million years old. Western Australia also has incredibly old rocks.

✳ LAYERS in time

The layers, or strata, of sedimentary rock may be horizontal when formed, owing to the downward pull of gravity. But over millions of years, enormous earth movements can tilt them at crazy angles and even tip them upside down. Working backwards from these angles today, experts can suggest how and where the layers first formed.

Rain and snow

Erosion Over millions of years, forces of nature such as rain, wind, ice, heat and cold gradually break apart and wear away even the hardest rocks.

Metamorphic rocks Huge heat and pressure near deep magma can change any kind of rock without melting it, into new types known as metamorphic rocks.

Metamorphosis zone

Sedimentary rock layers are often clearly visible along cliffs

Igneous rocks Great heat from the mantle can melt any rocks into liquid. When they cool, such as after erupting from a volcano, they solidify and form igneous rocks.

Navigate around an interactive diagram to reveal incredible photos of rocks by visiting www.factsforprojects.com and clicking on the web link.

The most common main rocks in the Earth's crust are all igneous. Basalt is the most common, forming oceanic plates.

Different kinds of rocks become molten at different temperatures. Some do so at 600°C. At 1200°C almost all rocks are molten.

1. A living thing dies and its hard parts are gradually covered by sediments

2. Over millions of years more layers of sediments build up and turn into solid rock

3. With more time the rock layers erode, revealing the fossils

Deposition Eroded rock particles form sediments that are washed out to sea by rivers. As the water speed slows, the particles settle or deposit as layers of sediments.

Currents slow as river reaches the sea

✳ How are FOSSILS formed?

Fossils are the remains of once-living things preserved in rocks and turned to stone. Usually, soft parts such as flesh or flowers rot away or are eaten. Only hard parts form fossils, such as animal bones, teeth, horns, claws and shells, and plant roots, wood, cones and pollen. The hard parts may be covered by sediments, on the seabed or a riverbank. Over a very long time more sediment layers build up and turn to stone. The parts inside the layers are also changed, keeping their shape but becoming part of the rock. Then earth movements, erosion and quarrying may expose the fossils at the surface.

Graded sediments As flowing water slows down, it drops its largest sediment particles first, such as pebbles and shingle. Then with further speed loss, smaller particles such as sand and mud settle.

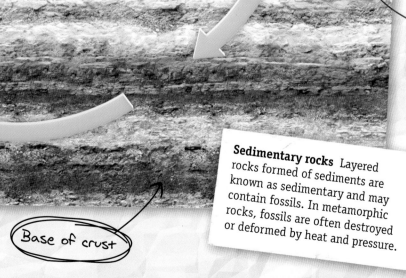

Sedimentary rocks Layered rocks formed of sediments are known as sedimentary and may contain fossils. In metamorphic rocks, fossils are often destroyed or deformed by heat and pressure.

Base of crust

Rocks vary hugely in their hardness and how well they resist erosion. Chalks are relatively soft, while granites are extremely tough and wear away very slowly.

VOLCANOES

Not all volcanoes are massive ground-shaking events that spurt out flying rocks and red-hot molten lava, as well as vast ash clouds and choking fumes. Some volcanoes ooze out their runny rocks much more slowly, over hundreds and thousands of years. But all volcanoes occur where the crust is too weak to hold in the high-pressure magma beneath.

Did you know?

The ten highest volcanic peaks above sea level are all in the Andes mountains of South America. Tallest is Ojos del Salado ('Eyes of Salt') on the border between Chile and Argentina, at 6891 metres.

Ash and fumes Small ash particles can rise tens of kilometres into the air. Choking sulphur-rich fumes may suffocate animals and people.

A dormant volcano is 'sleeping' but may erupt again. An extinct one is 'dead' and unlikely to erupt again.

Volcanic bomb

Dense ash

✳ CHAOS in the SKIES

In April 2010 a smallish volcano in Iceland, called Eyjafjallajökull, began to pour out ash and vapour. The amounts of lava and other material were small, but the great ash clouds rose to heights of 9 kilometres and drifted across northern Europe. Aircraft were soon grounded, not so much because pilots couldn't see, but because of the possible damage caused by ash particles if they were sucked into the engines. The shutdown lasted for several days and millions of people had to abandon their travel plans.

Parasitic cones The magma in the main conduit may 'eat' its way through the main volcano cone like a red-hot lance, to form smaller parasitic cones which erupt on the sides.

Magma chamber The red-hot molten rock is under enormous pressure and finds the weakest place above for its eruption.

In 2010, ash from an Icelandic volcano caused air traffic chaos

To learn more about volcanoes, and to build your own volcano and watch it erupt, visit www.factsforprojects.com and click on the web link.

Throat, vent and crater The conduit usually widens near the top into the throat, then opens at the vent, which is surrounded by the solid rock of the crater.

Molten rock is called magma until it emerges at the surface, when it becomes lava.

Lava flows downhill as it cools

Conduit Also called the pipe or chimney, this is the main channel for magma as it spurts from the chamber up towards the surface.

✳ FLAT or TALL?

The shape of a volcano depends on the type of lava that emerges, and its temperature. Very high temperatures (1200°C) for a rock with a low melting point mean the lava is very runny. It spreads rapidly before it cools and solidifies, forming a low, gently sloping shield volcano. Lower temperatures, perhaps less than 800°C, for a high melting point rock, produce thick or viscous lava. This cools and solidifies rapidly and so repeated eruptions build up a tall cone shape.

SHIELD VOLCANO

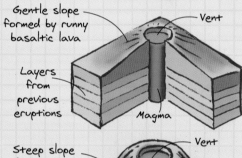

Gentle slope formed by runny basaltic lava

Vent

Layers from previous eruptions

Magma

Steep slope from thick, fast-cooling lava

Vent

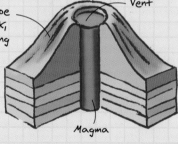

Magma

CONE VOLCANO

Volcanic bomb The volcano's force may hurl huge lumps of glowing rock, some bigger than cars, many hundreds of metres. As they fly through the air they may take on a smooth shape like teardrops.

MOUNTAIN BUILDING

The great peaks and ridges of mountains rise above lowlands in several ways. They can be built by volcanoes, especially by several eruptions over a long time. Two tectonic plates may collide so their edges crumple and buckle into fold mountains. Giant blocks of crust can slip against each other, with one forced higher. Or relentless erosion can wear away some of an upland area to leave peaks of the most resistant rocks.

Did you know?

The world's greatest mountain range, the Himalayas, began when the Indian and Eurasian tectonic plates started to collide 50 million years ago (see opposite). These mountains are still growing by five millimetres each year.

Scarp Where one block tilts as it slips against another, a long steep slope called a scarp (escarpment) is the result. The up-moving block is called the horst, and the one going down is known as the graben.

Graben (dropped block)

The Zanskar Range in India shows sharp-edged peaks

✳ SHARP to SMOOTH

Often, the aerial view of a mountain range shows whether it is young or old. The newest mountains tend to have tall, sharp, jagged ridges and peaks. Over time these are worn by erosion and become more rounded and smooth. The newest parts of the Himalayas, such as the Zanskar Range, show this topography (three-dimensional shape), as do the Alps in Europe. The Urals between Europe and Asia are older, lower and rounded. The Appalachians of eastern North America are also very old and worn – about 400 million years ago they would have looked like the Himalayas today.

BLOCK-FAULT

Slipping blocks Along a crack or fault, one huge lump or block of rock may slip up or down in relation to its neighbour. This can happen suddenly, during an earthquake, or gradually over thousands of years.

The Usas Scarp on Antarctica is over 300 km long – but hidden under deep snow. It was only discovered in 1940.

Pulling apart At some faults (giant cracks) the blocks of rock on either side pull apart due to tensional or stretching forces. The middle sections begin to slip down, leaving high ground on either side.

The East African Rift is a massive crack in the African plate where it is splitting into two smaller plates.

Test your knowledge of mountains with a quiz by visiting
www.factsforprojects.com and clicking on the web link.

Much of
Europe's River
Rhine flows in
a long, narrow,
down-slipped
graben.

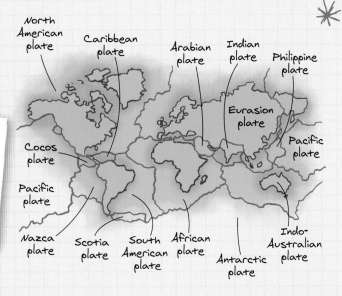

North
American
plate

Caribbean
plate

Arabian
plate

Indian
plate

Philippine
plate

Eurasion
plate

Pacific
plate

Cocos
plate

Pacific
plate

Nazca
plate

Scotia
plate

South
American
plate

African
plate

Antarctic
plate

Indo-
Australian
plate

✳ How PLATES make MOUNTAINS

Drifting tectonic plates are the most powerful mountain-builders, but the process takes millions of years. As explained opposite, the Himalayas are the result of the colossal forces where the Indian and Eurasian plates ram into each other. The Andes Mountains in western South America, the world's second-biggest range, have risen where the Nazca plate and part of the Antarctic plate are sliding under the South American plate. Because this is a subduction zone, the gigantic peaks are also volcanoes.

Rift valley Where the land sinks along the fault, a rift valley forms. There may be several sets of steep cliffs along its sides.

RIFT FAULT

Magma As the rock blocks slide away from each other, this may allow magma to well up between them from far below. There may be geysers or hot springs, bubbling mud pools and even small volcanic eruptions along slit-like fissures.

The greatest depth of the East African Rift is more than 1400 m, on the bottom of Lake Tanganyika.

Steep slopes
along plate edge

SUBDUCTION

Continental collision Where two continental tectonic plates push together, if one is thinner or less rigid than the other, it may slide below.

Steep edge As the thinner, more flexible plate rubs underneath, it can crack and rumple the edge of its neighbour into mountains.

GLACIERS

In the mountains, noises like gunshots sometimes echo among the peaks. These are the sounds of a giant ribbon of ice cracking as it bends, buckles and slides slowly downhill, gradually and relentlessly. This 'frozen river' is known as a glacier. It is renewed at its upper end by fresh snowfall, and disappears at its lower end by melting or as chunks that split off into the sea.

Did you know?

One of the main signs of global warming is the 'retreat' of glaciers, as rising temperatures cause their lower ends to melt at an increasing rate. In Antarctica more than 300 glaciers have been melting back in recent years, some by more than 50 metres each year.

More than two-thirds of the world's fresh water is locked up in glaciers and similar ice formations.

Cirque outlet

✳ When ICE MELTS

During the last Great Ice Age, which started 110,000 years ago, ice sheets and glaciers covered vast areas of land, especially in northern regions. As the glaciers flowed downhill they carved giant gouges into the rocks. When the Ice Age began to fade around 11,000 years ago, the glaciers melted away to leave the gouges clear, as valleys. A glacial valley has a U-shaped profile or cross-section, with a gently rounded bottom. Valleys worn away by rivers tend to be V-shaped with a steep angle at the base.

Medial moraine This ribbon of rock fragments near the middle of the glacier usually occurs after two lateral (edge) moraines join higher up the valley.

Compressed ice surface

If all the glaciers and other ice on the land suddenly melted, the global sea level would rise by more than 70 metres.

Ice at the base of some glaciers in Canada is more than 100,000 years old.

Snout (nose) The glacier gradually melts here. The snout's position depends partly on air temperature, which rises as the glacier comes down to lower altitude.

Beautiful U-shaped valleys were created by glaciers

To see spectacular aerial images of glaciers around the world visit www.factsforprojects.com and click on the web link.

Cirques These are bowl-like depressions high up the valley, where snow falls and is blown from the surrounding steep slopes, and compresses into ice. They are the main 'feed' for the glacier.

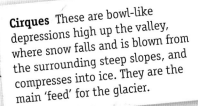

In the 1950s, the Kutiah Glacier in Pakistan travelled more than 110 m each day for several months. However, its rate then slowed.

Heavily eroded valley sides

Lateral moraine
This is bits of stone and rock rubbed off the side of the valley, visible as a long side stripe, as the glacier gouges past.

Transverse crevasses
Where the glacier moves over undulations in the slope, or melts at the end, these crosswise cracks appear.

✳ EXTREME forces

Each glacier has its own shape and pattern of crevasses, moraines and other features, depending on the slope of the underlying valley, type of rocks, amount of snowfall, temperature and other conditions. For example, longitudinal crevasses run lengthways along the glacier, parallel to its flow direction. They tend to form where the valley becomes wider, and the glacier flattens and stretches sideways. Moraines at the surface appear where the ice in the glacier rises as it flows.

Rock fragments are carried to the surface of the glacier

Transverse crevasses

Melting nose or snout

Outwash gravel

Rock fragments are broken and scraped from the bedrock

Bedrock

Meltwater Varying from small puddles to a large lake, the melted ice fills the ground at the snout and then drains away as a stream.

Antarctica's Lambert Glacier is more than 400 km long and 100 km wide at its broadest.

Terminal moraine Bits of rock in the moraines, known as glacial till, melt out and pile up at the snout. If the snout moves with climate change, the terminal moraine is spread out.

U-shaped valley where glacier has melted back

CAVES

Not all rocks are 'waterproof'. Some are worn away by rain water trickling into their tiny cracks and crevices. The water may contain natural chemicals that turn it into a very weak acid. It dissolves the rock, enlarging the cracks. This chemical reaction particularly affects limestone. Over millions of years it can create underground wonderlands of caves and tunnels.

Did you know?

Mammoth Cave is a national park in Kentucky, USA, with a total length of caverns and tunnels that exceeds 620 kilometres. This is the discovered and surveyed length so far. In the future, detailed exploration may reveal yet more passages to study and map.

The Vrtoglavica Cave in Slovenia, near the Italian border, has a single vertical shaft more than 600 m deep.

Swallow hole and shaft

✳ Underground WORLD

Beautiful hanging stalactites, up-pointing stalagmites and similar cave formations take a very long time to enlarge. Typically they lengthen by 0.1 to 0.2 millimetres per year, although some grow 20 times faster, depending on the speed of the water flow, the amounts of dissolved minerals and the temperature. Jeitta Grotto Caves in Lebanon contain a stalactite more than 8 metres long, and probably at least 50,000 years of age, while the Gruta Rei de Moto Cave in Brazil has several columns taller than 20 metres.

Dry cavern This cave area was once almost flooded, with an underground lake and stream. But earth movements have raised the rocks and lowered the water table, so it is now mostly dry.

Voronya Cave in Georgia is more than 2100 m deep from its opening to its lowest passages.

Speleothems This is the overall name for rock shapes formed in caves by water dissolving, moving and then evaporating to leave mineral deposits. As well as stalactites and stalagmites, there are flowstones shaped like curtains or drapes.

Underground stream After rainwater pours down sinkholes or seeps through the rocks, it collects in pools and lakes, or joins an underground river system.

Spectacular cave formations are thousands of years old

Find out how you can grow your own stalactite by visiting www.factsforprojects.com and clicking on the web link.

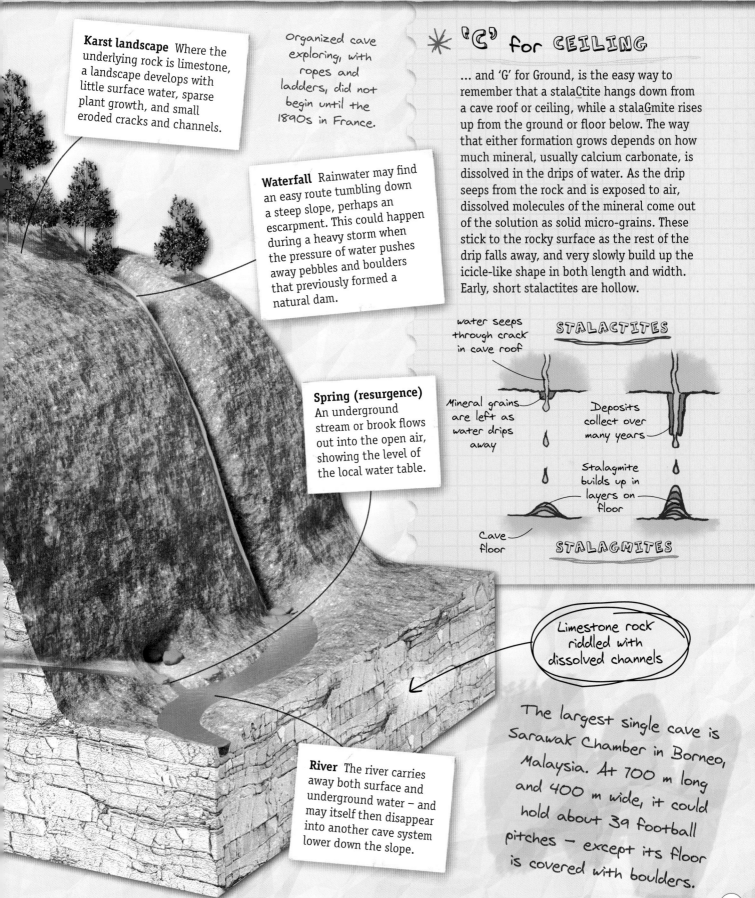

Karst landscape Where the underlying rock is limestone, a landscape develops with little surface water, sparse plant growth, and small eroded cracks and channels.

Organized cave exploring, with ropes and ladders, did not begin until the 1890s in France.

Waterfall Rainwater may find an easy route tumbling down a steep slope, perhaps an escarpment. This could happen during a heavy storm when the pressure of water pushes away pebbles and boulders that previously formed a natural dam.

Spring (resurgence) An underground stream or brook flows out into the open air, showing the level of the local water table.

River The river carries away both surface and underground water – and may itself then disappear into another cave system lower down the slope.

✳ "C" for CEILING

... and 'G' for Ground, is the easy way to remember that a stalaCtite hangs down from a cave roof or ceiling, while a stalaGmite rises up from the ground or floor below. The way that either formation grows depends on how much mineral, usually calcium carbonate, is dissolved in the drips of water. As the drip seeps from the rock and is exposed to air, dissolved molecules of the mineral come out of the solution as solid micro-grains. These stick to the rocky surface as the rest of the drip falls away, and very slowly build up the icicle-like shape in both length and width. Early, short stalactites are hollow.

water seeps through crack in cave roof

STALACTITES

Mineral grains are left as water drips away

Deposits collect over many years

Stalagmite builds up in layers on floor

Cave floor

STALAGMITES

Limestone rock riddled with dissolved channels

The largest single cave is Sarawak Chamber in Borneo, Malaysia. At 700 m long and 400 m wide, it could hold about 39 football pitches – except its floor is covered with boulders.

GEYSERS & HOT SPRINGS

Every 90 minutes or so in Yellowstone National Park, USA, 'Old Faithful' erupts. A jet of 30,000 litres of hot water and a fierce cloud of steam spurt up to 50 metres high for as long as five minutes. This is one of the world's best-known geysers – explosive eruptions of superheated water and vapour from a hole or vent in the surface rocks, heated by hot rocks far below.

Did you know?

Many geysers are near areas of volcanic activity, in places such as Chile, Iceland, Japan and New Zealand. About half of the world's 1000 or so active geysers are in Yellowstone Park, which shows no volcanic signs at present. However it is the site of a supervolcano that may at some point erupt.

Erupted material
A geyser's 'steam' is scalding-hot droplets of water carried aloft by a rush of water vapour – the gaseous form of water – which by itself is invisible. There may also be sulphur-rich fumes.

✳ A natural ENERGY SOURCE

If incredibly hot molten rock or magma is relatively near the surface, perhaps just a few hundred metres down, then hot springs, geysers and similar formations occur at the surface. These represent heat or thermal energy waiting to be used. The hot springs are used to heat buildings and clean water supplies. Also in places such as California, the Philippines, Iceland and Japan, water is circulated through pipes installed in boreholes drilled down into the hot rocks. The water carries the intense heat up to the surface for generating electricity in geothermal power stations.

Water sources The geyser's water supply comes from rain, snow, and often also nearby rivers and lakes.

Layers of 'geyserite' minerals

Yellowstone's Steamboat Geyser is currently the world's highest, at up to 90 metres. Yet it did not erupt at all for 50 years, between 1911 and 1961.

Magma or hot rocks
The heat source for the geyser is on average 1000 to 2000 metres below the surface. Depending on the local rock types, water may take thousands of years to seep or percolate this deep.

As well as creating electricity, geysers and hot springs make bathing fun

To find out more about spectacular geysers and hot springs visit www.factsforprojects.com and click on the web link.

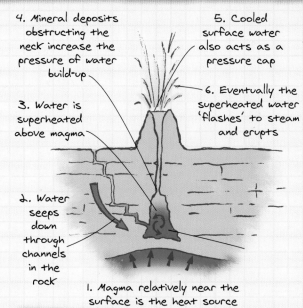

4. Mineral deposits obstructing the neck increase the pressure of water build-up

5. Cooled surface water also acts as a pressure cap

3. Water is superheated above magma

6. Eventually the superheated water 'flashes' to steam and erupts

2. Water seeps down through channels in the rock

1. Magma relatively near the surface is the heat source

The GEYSER cycle

Each geyser has its own pattern of eruption times and volumes. Some have a regular cycle, with a steady supply of groundwater in the rocks. Others are not at all regular. They may rely on rainfall that has seeped in from a small area, and so during dry spells, they erupt less often. Also the main vent leading up from the water chamber may become blocked or narrowed by mineral deposits. This means a longer recharge time, until the pressure has increased enough to blast out the water and vapours. If the narrowing is shot away by the blast, then less pressure is needed, so the next eruption is sooner but less powerful.

Geyser cone As the erupting water suddenly loses pressure and cools, minerals come out of the solution and build up layers to form a volcano-like sinter cone.

Fine volcanic-ash soil

Mud pot Also called a mud pool, heated water flows up steadily from this opening like a hot spring. It stirs the fine soil particles into a pale slurry, often with bubbling sulphur fumes, giving a 'rotten eggs' smell.

Waimangu Geyser near Rotorua, New Zealand, reportedly erupted to heights greater than 450 m. But it only lasted for four years until 1904, when a local landslide made it extinct.

Solid rock above magma

Reservoir (water chamber) The reservoir may be one or a few large hollow chambers in the rocks, or a network of much smaller spaces, more like a stone sponge. Rising pressure due to the heat is transmitted through all of the reservoir.

Waimangu Geyser was so powerful that in 1903 one of its eruptions killed four people. Despite several warnings, they ventured too close and were blasted to death.

ISLANDS & ATOLLS

Across the tropical oceans, circular or C-shaped islands just about break the surface of the sparkling blue sea, enclosing a shallow lagoon where the water is calm and warm. These islands are atolls, built by a combination of volcanic eruptions and the growth of rocky coral reefs due to tiny creatures known as polyps. The tip of the original volcano may be visible in the lagoon, or it may have sunk beneath the waves.

Did you know?

The formation of tropical atolls from volcanic islands was first explained by English naturalist Charles Darwin, who also proposed the theory of evolution by natural selection in 1859. He worked out the process on his round-the-world trip on the sailing ship *Beagle*, from 1831 to 1836, and wrote his report on the process in 1842.

The largest atoll is the Great Chagos Bank in the Indian Ocean, where lagoons and lands cover more than 12,000 sq km.

Coral reefs cover less than 1/1000 of the surface area of the oceans. Yet they are home to more than one-quarter of all species of sea animals.

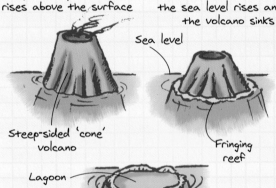

1. A seabed volcano erupts many times and rises above the surface

Steep-sided 'cone' volcano

2. Coral reefs form at the surface, meanwhile the sea level rises and/or the volcano sinks

Sea level

Fringing reef

Lagoon

3. The reefs grow up as the cone sinks down, eventually leaving a ring-shaped atoll

Australia's Great Barrier Reef, which extends for 2500 km, is made up of nearly 3000 small reefs and 1000 islands.

Gap in reef caused by storm

Barrier reef This atoll is half-formed, with a gap developing between the main island and the coral structure. It has passed through the fringing reef stage and is now known as a barrier reef.

How do ATOLLS form?

Many volcanoes erupt on the seabed. Some of them become tall enough to break the surface as small islands – especially in the Pacific Ocean, which has much volcanic activity. As the eruptions fade, coral animals start to build reefs in the shallows around the island's shores. Then great earth movements cause the seafloor to subside, or – as happened after the last great Ice Age – melting ice raises the sea level. As the original volcanic island slowly sinks out of sight, the corals keep pace and continue to build their reefs so their tops stay at sea level.

Accumulated reef material The original fringing reef stage, where the coral structure was attached to the main island, now lies buried perhaps hundreds of metres down.

To see some brilliant photos of the Maldives atolls visit www.factsforprojects.com and click on the web link.

Nukuoro is an atoll in the Pacific Ocean that has more than 40 islets on an almost perfect circular reef, surrounding a lagoon almost 6 km across.

In DANGER

Low-lying atolls and similar coral formations are among the areas most threatened by global warming. As ice sheets and glaciers melt and raise sea levels, even by a few tens of centimetres, these atolls will be in increasing danger from wave action and soil destruction due to salt water. In the middle of the Pacific Ocean, the island nation of Kiribati (Gilbert and Christmas islands) may be the first country to disappear due to global warming. Its 32 main coral atolls are only a few metres above sea level. However, there are recent signs that the coral reefs are growing in height to keep pace with the rising water.

Serene tropical atolls are in danger from global warming

Reef growth Coral animals need sunlight to thrive, for the plant-like microbes that grow inside them. So as the volcano sinks, they build on top of previous generations of corals in order to stay in warm, sunlit, shallow water.

Extinct volcano crater Lava and fumes pouring from the active volcano made the island too dangerous for life. But since it went extinct, vegetation has been able to grow on its slopes and support animal life, especially birds.

Rough water of open sea

Lagoon The sheltered central lagoon is an ideal place for sea animals to breed, so their young are away from the predators and dangers of the open ocean.

RIVERS

Each river has a 'life' of its own. It is born or begins in the highlands, as small streams that tumble down steep slopes and come together to form the main course. As the slope lessens the river slows down and reaches middle age, winding or meandering across the flatter lowlands. Finally it reaches old age and widens at its mouth, or estuary, to disappear into the sea.

Did you know?

There have been many arguments about whether the Nile or the Amazon is the longest river – it depends where you define the start or source. But there is no argument about river size. The Amazon pours more water into the ocean than the next six-biggest rivers combined.

The Amazon River accounts for one-fifth of the world's total river water. New sources were discovered in 2001, 2007 and 2008.

The Nile River is 6650 km long. Much of its course is through the Sahara Desert.

Tributaries from coastal range of hills

The Amazon is more than 6400 km long.

River meanders as it flows over flat ground

Silt deposits indicate previous river course

Fast flowing water on outside of bend erodes bank

River's new course

Slow flowing water deposits sediments on inside of bend

Erosion

Eventually erosion leads to a new course, leaving the oxbow lake

✳ How OXBOW LAKES form

As a river flows around a bend, it moves faster on the outside of the curve, wearing away the bank at a greater rate. The water on the inside of the bend flows slower, perhaps slowly enough to allow any sediments, such as sand or silt, to settle as banks. This process increases the angle of the curve until the river breaks through a 'short cut' and takes a new course. The former bend or meander is left isolated as a U- or even C-shaped lake. These lakes are known as oxbows, from the shape of the yoke used for oxen pulling wagons or ploughs. In Australia they are called billabongs – a term derived from an Aboriginal expression for 'dead water'.

Delta On the left side of this delta is the greenery of a saltmarsh, where specialized plants gain a roothold. The right side has the shifting patchwork of channels and mounds that are mudflats.

Read more about the Nile and Amazon rivers, and how they compare by visiting www.factsforprojects.com and clicking on the web link.

Waterfall Where the river flows over the edge of a hard section of rock, onto some less resistant rocks, it gradually wears away the latter to form a waterfall.

Sources Warm, moist sea air rises over the mountains, cools, and its water vapour condenses into droplets of clouds and rain. Rainfall creates streams and brooks.

Rapids A relatively steep part of the slope over resistant rocks makes the water flow fast, with boulders and outcrops visible at the surface.

Meanders As the slope lessens the river begins to 'wander' to and fro. It finds the course of least resistance around gentle undulations on the plain.

Oxbow lake Formed by the process shown opposite, these lakes indicate the earlier meanders of the main river. In time they may fill with sediment – or perhaps become the main course again.

The UK's fastest river is the Spey in Scotland, with an average speed of 16 m per second.

✳ DELTAS on the MOVE

Around the world, huge rivers are expanding their deltas into the ocean, as deposits of sand, mud and silt extend seawards. The Mississippi River Delta in the southern USA has enlarged in the past by up to 100 metres each year. But a strong storm such as 2005's Hurricane Katrina can wash away huge amounts and put back the delta's growth by many decades. In fact the Mississippi River Delta may soon start to shrink again. The many dams and levees (raised banks) along the river's course trap sediments far upstream, so now not enough reaches the delta to maintain its size.

The Amazon's estuary is up to 80 km wide.

Delta channels through mud and silt change every few years

COASTAL FEATURES

Coasts and shores are some of the best places to see erosion in action. A great storm can transform the scene in a few hours as huge waves smash into and collapse cliffs, move car-sized boulders, and wash away shingle spits, sand beaches and mudflats. The relentless wind helps as it blows sand grains against rocks and erodes strange shapes.

Did you know?

In the far southeast of Bangladesh, Cox's Bazar lays claim to the world's longest natural continuous beach, at almost 125 kilometres. It contains an estimated 25 million tonnes of sand and other sediments. The USA's famous Long Beach, in the north west state of Washington, is a mere 45 kilometres in length.

Ball's Pyramid, near Australia's Lord Howe island, is the tallest sea stack at 562 m.

Sea stack The most resistant areas of an old, heavily eroded headland remain as tall, isolated columns of points known as sea stacks.

Peaceful sandy bays can be ideal spots for safe bathing

Mangrove swamp Along sheltered warmer shores, mangrove trees grow into the tidal shallows. Their roots are specialized to cope with salt water and thick mud.

Mudflats Any floating mud particles brought onto the coast are transported by longshore drift (see opposite) to the calm end of the bay, where they settle.

✳ Sun, sea, sand, SAFETY

Millions of people flock to the coasts to enjoy swimming, sunbathing and sports ranging from water-skiing to para-gliding. But coasts also claim many lives each year. One great hazard on a very wide, flat beach is being cut off by the incoming tide, as the water races in faster than a person can run. Fierce currents can also drag bathers out to sea. Much less common dangers are being bitten or stung by animals such as jellyfish, coneshells and stonefish. Rarest of all are shark attacks.

Find out more about the parts of a coastline and cliff formation by visiting www.factsforprojects.com and clicking on the web link.

Arch Waves coming in at an angle wear away the softer parts of the cliff and may even erode a hole to form a coastal arch.

Resistant rocks of headland

Cliff The steepness of a cliff depends on the type of rock and the power of the incoming waves whipped up by the wind. Lower levels are eroded and undercut by waves, then the upper parts collapse, and so on.

Maujit Qagarssuasia, or Thumbnail Cliffs, in southern Greenland, fall almost vertically 1550 m to the North Atlantic Ocean.

Cave formed at high tide mark

Beach The tides, currents and wave action here are strong enough to remove tiny mud and silt particles, but not larger sand grains.

The Arabat Spit in the Azov Sea, part of the Black Sea in Eastern Europe, is 110 km long with an average width of 3.5 km.

✳ What is LONGSHORE DRIFT?

Winds rarely blow at right angles directly from the sea onto the shore. They usually come in at an angle to the shore, and make waves that do the same. As each wave swishes onto the shore it pushes sediments, such as shingle, sand or mud, up and along the shore slightly. The retreating wave allows the sediments to roll back straight down towards the sea. In this way the waves move the sediments in a zig-zag path along the coast, which is known as longshore drift. The transported particles can form sand bars and shingle spits.

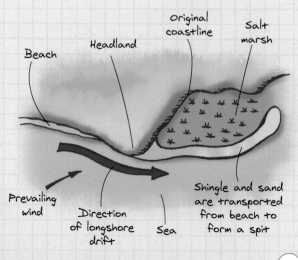

Original coastline

Salt marsh

Beach

Headland

Prevailing wind

Direction of longshore drift

Sea

Shingle and sand are transported from beach to form a spit

OCEAN FLOOR

The bottom of the sea covers more than twice the area covered by all land on Earth. This vast expanse has even more varied features than the land, with hills and valleys, wide flat plains covered by rocks or mud, sheer cliffs, tall mountains, and plunging, canyon-like deep-sea trenches. The ocean floor is shaped by enormous forces including deep-sea currents, volcanoes and the movement of vast tectonic plates.

Did you know?

The Grand Canyon in Arizona, USA, is up to 1800 metres deep. However, the Marianas Trench in the west Pacific Ocean goes down more than 10,000 metres. It has one slot-shaped canyon in it, the Challenger Deep, which is 10,970 metres below the surface.

 ## Deep-sea FOOD

For many years, explorers believed that life was sparse on many parts of the ocean floor. With the discovery of hydrothermal vents, and whale falls in the 1980s, these ideas have changed. A whale fall is the carcass of a great whale that has sunk to the seabed. Here it becomes a giant meal for all kinds of weird creatures, from sleeper sharks to bone-eating snot worms. In cold water the slow-rotting carcass may feed creatures for up to 100 years.

The average width of continental shelves is 80 km.

Run-off Rivers bring sand, mud, silt and other sediments to the ocean, which are then mixed up and swept away by currents and tides, out to deeper areas.

Continental shelf This zone of shallow water, 100–150 m deep, surrounds most continents. It is usually rich in nutrients and receives plentiful sunlight, and so teems with life.

Continental slope The continental shelf dips down steeply here, marking the edge of the continental tectonic plate and giving way to the oceanic plate.

Mid-oceanic ridge Two diverging (moving apart) tectonic plates allow magma from below to well up as lava and harden, adding new seafloor rock to the edges of the plates at a long underwater ridge.

A rotting whale carcass can provide food for many years

Continental shelves cover one-twelfth of the total ocean area, but contain up to one-third of ocean life.

Watch a video of a volcano erupting on the Pacific Ocean floor by visiting www.factsforprojects.com and clicking on the web link.

Due to the spreading seafloor, the Atlantic Ocean is widening at a rate of 2–2.5 cm each year.

Movement of seafloor

Nodules can cover vast areas of the ocean floor

Layers built up over many millions of years

✳ NATURAL nodules

Here and there on the ocean floor are piles of potato-sized rounded lumps of minerals, called manganese nodules. They are rich in metals such as manganese and iron, plus other minerals. These come out of solution from sea water and form in layers around a small 'core' such as the tiny shell of a sea creature or even a shark's tooth. The process is called concretion and is similar to the way pearls grow in oysters. It needs special conditions of water flow and temperature and happens very slowly, over millions of years.

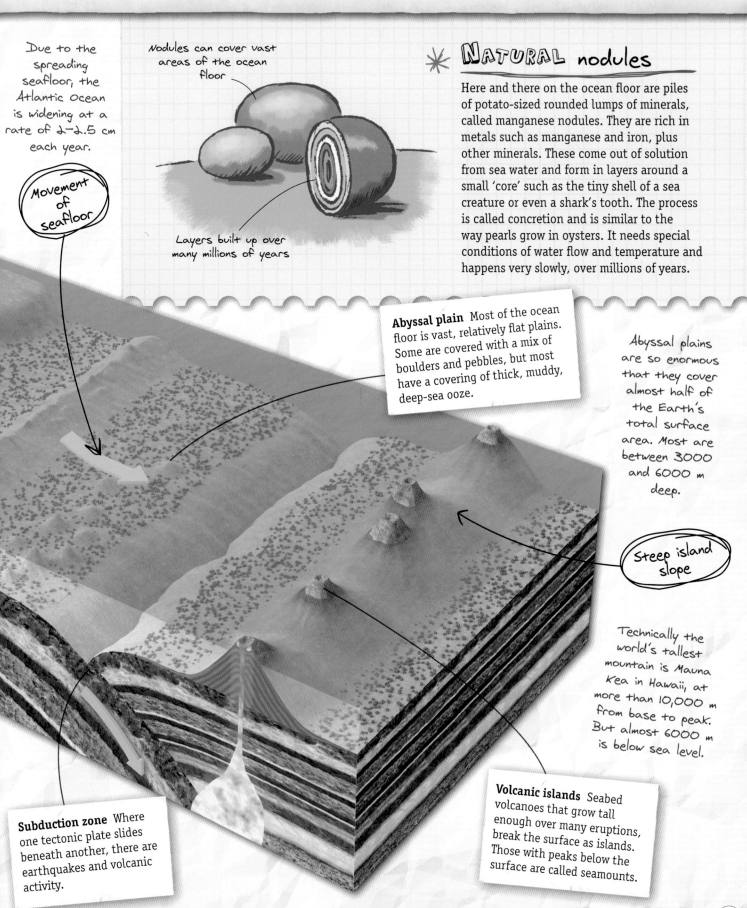

Abyssal plain Most of the ocean floor is vast, relatively flat plains. Some are covered with a mix of boulders and pebbles, but most have a covering of thick, muddy, deep-sea ooze.

Abyssal plains are so enormous that they cover almost half of the Earth's total surface area. Most are between 3000 and 6000 m deep.

Steep island slope

Technically the world's tallest mountain is Mauna Kea in Hawaii, at more than 10,000 m from base to peak. But almost 6000 m is below sea level.

Subduction zone Where one tectonic plate slides beneath another, there are earthquakes and volcanic activity.

Volcanic islands Seabed volcanoes that grow tall enough over many eruptions, break the surface as islands. Those with peaks below the surface are called seamounts.

HYDROTHERMAL VENTS

In 1977 the submersible Alvin dived more than 2000 metres into the Pacific Ocean near the Galapagos Islands. It surveyed an amazing and unexpected sight – superhot water, laden with dissolved minerals, spurting from cracks and tall chimney-like structures in the ocean floor. Around the hot-water cracks, or hydrothermal vents, thrived an amazing array of bizarre creatures seen nowhere else on Earth.

Did you know?

The discovery of hydrothermal vents made scientists change their ideas about life on Earth. The life-forms here do not depend ultimately on the Sun, like the plants and animals at the surface. In fact, life on Earth may have begun down here, deep in the primeval seas.

Chimney (stack) Minerals suddenly precipitating (coming out of solution) add to the rim of the chimney as it grows taller. Some vent chimneys are more than 50 m high.

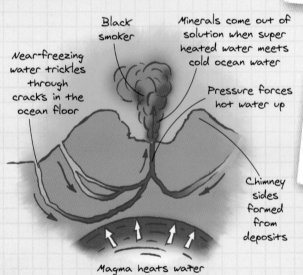

Black smoker

Minerals come out of solution when super heated water meets cold ocean water

Near-freezing water trickles through cracks in the ocean floor

Pressure forces hot water up

Chimney sides formed from deposits

Magma heats water

Superheated water The water temperature is usually more than 100°C and may be as high as 460°C, over four times its normal boiling point.

✳ How do BLACK SMOKERS work?

Black smokers and other deep-sea vents are similar in some ways to geysers. Cold ocean water trickles down through cracks in the seabed and meets very hot rocks warmed by magma (molten rock) relatively close beneath. The water becomes superheated above its normal boiling point because it is under so much pressure, and is able to dissolve plentiful minerals from the rocks. As it gets even hotter it is forced up a slit or pipe, the chimney, back to the ocean floor.

Feed water The deep ocean floor water is close to freezing, usually 2–4°C. Immense pressure forces it down through channels and cracks in the seabed.

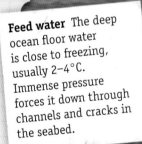

Find facts, pictures and incredible videos of hydrothermal vents by visiting www.factsforprojects.com and clicking on the web link.

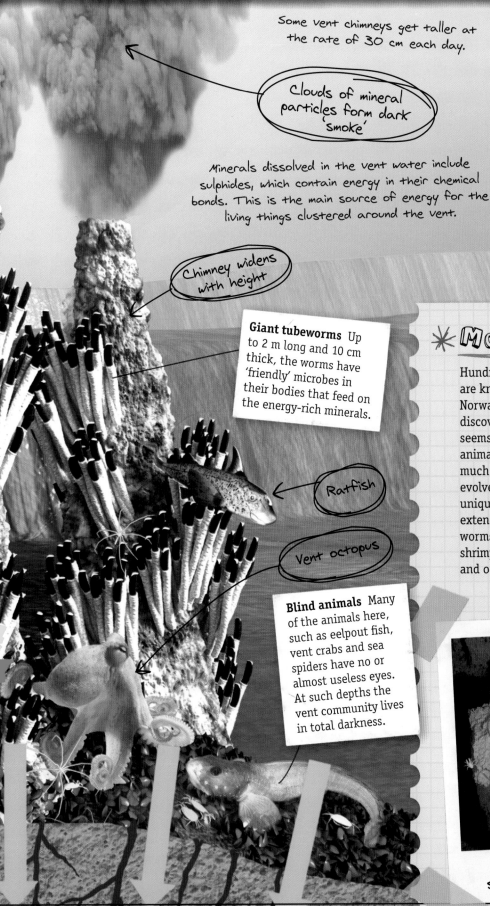

Some vent chimneys get taller at the rate of 30 cm each day.

Clouds of mineral particles form dark 'smoke'

Minerals dissolved in the vent water include sulphides, which contain energy in their chemical bonds. This is the main source of energy for the living things clustered around the vent.

In 2008 black smokers were discovered in the North Atlantic Ocean between Greenland and Norway. This was much further north than many scientists believed they could exist.

Chimney widens with height

Giant tubeworms Up to 2 m long and 10 cm thick, the worms have 'friendly' microbes in their bodies that feed on the energy-rich minerals.

Ratfish

Vent octopus

Blind animals Many of the animals here, such as eelpout fish, vent crabs and sea spiders have no or almost useless eyes. At such depths the vent community lives in total darkness.

✳ MONSTERS below

Hundreds of deep-sea hydrothermal vents are known, from the northern seas near Norway and Alaska, to the tropics. More are discovered almost every year, and each region seems to have its own specialized types of animals. These have evolved in isolation, much as land plants and animals on islands evolve in their own separate habitats, into unique species. The list of vent creatures extends from giant tubeworms and other worms to fish such as eelpouts, crabs and shrimp, shellfish like clams and sea snails, and octopus and squid.

A community of vent crabs scuttles about in the darkness

HURRICANES

The words 'hurricane' and 'typhoon' can strike fear into the hearts of people living near oceans in warmer regions. These giant weather systems, known as tropical cyclones, cause some of the greatest natural disasters. They build in power over the sea, then fierce winds and torrential rain pound coasts and islands, and cause destruction hundreds of kilometres inland.

Did you know?

Hurricanes and typhoons are given names to make them easy to identify and remember. The annual list for hurricanes has a mix of names, male and female, from different ethnic origins, starting with A for the first of the season, then B, C and so on. The lists repeat every six years.

Cloud ceiling

Hurricanes that cause huge amounts of damage have their names 'retired' or removed from the official lists. This happened to Andrew in 1992 and Katrina in 2005.

Rainfall Many centimetres of rain can fall in a few hours around the eye of the storm. In 1988, Hurricane Mitch unleashed 2 m of rainfall over three days.

The Earth's own spinning forces mean hurricanes tend to move in a westerly direction.

Rotation General wind patterns in the area, plus the Coriolis Force due to the Earth's rotation, usually start the whole hurricane spinning slowly.

Rising warm air from sea

✳ BLOWN away

In 2005, Hurricane Katrina hit the coast of the USA from Florida to Texas, causing most damage in Louisiana. More than 1800 people died in the costliest natural disaster ever to affect the USA. In 2008, Cyclone Nargis devastated huge low-lying areas of Burma (Myanmar) and resulted in at least 138,000 deaths – the country's authorities stopped counting at this number. In these disasters, as well as fatalities and damage to buildings, the waves and floods of seawater soak into vast areas of rich farmland near the coast. The salt gets into the soil and ruins farmland for many years.

Hurricane Katrina caused most of the US city of New Orleans to flood

To find out how a small storm grows into a giant hurricane visit www.factsforprojects.com and click on the web link.

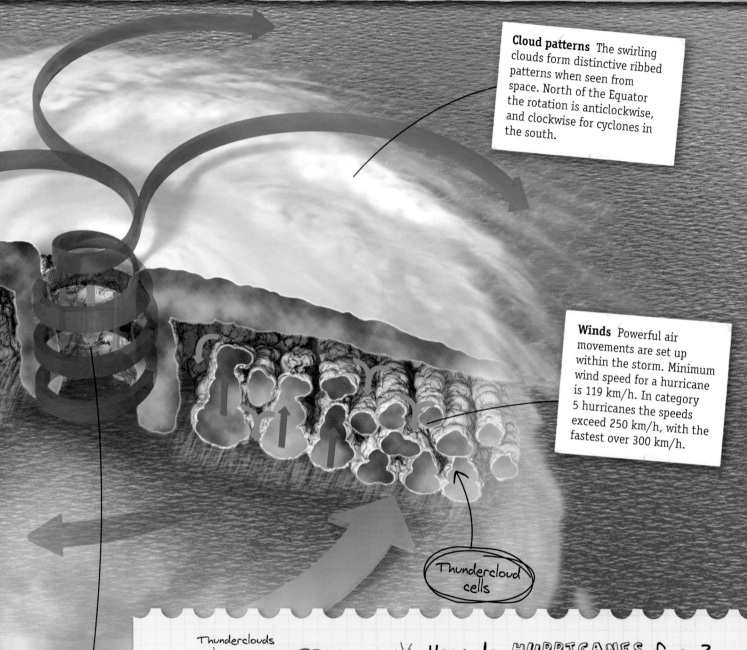

Cloud patterns The swirling clouds form distinctive ribbed patterns when seen from space. North of the Equator the rotation is anticlockwise, and clockwise for cyclones in the south.

Winds Powerful air movements are set up within the storm. Minimum wind speed for a hurricane is 119 km/h. In category 5 hurricanes the speeds exceed 250 km/h, with the fastest over 300 km/h.

Thundercloud cells

Eye of the storm
The eye has the lowest pressure and is relatively calm, with no rain and even clear skies. It, and the whole storm, move along at speeds sometimes reaching 100 km/h.

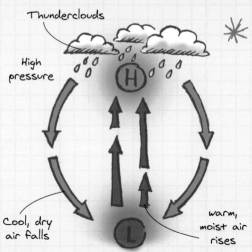

Thunderclouds

High pressure

H

Cool, dry air falls

warm, moist air rises

L

Low pressure in eye

✳ How do HURRICANES form?

A hurricane or cyclone needs special conditions of atmospheric pressure, temperature, local wind speed and pattern, and amounts of water vapour in the air. The warmed ocean surface heats the air above, which becomes lighter and rises. This air contains great quantities of water vapour due to evaporation from the sea. The rising air cools, its vapour condenses as clouds and rain, and it falls. This sets up movements called convection currents that spread to neighbouring areas of the atmosphere. Meanwhile, wind patterns and the Earth's rotation set the whole storm spinning.

GLOSSARY

Atoll

An island, usually made from a coral reef or reefs, with a lagoon (area of water) inside. Some atolls are complete rings above the surface, others are C- or U-shaped.

Cirque

The bowl-like upper end of a valley, usually filled with snow and ice, which feeds a glacier that flows down the valley.

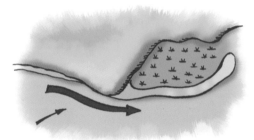

Longshore drift

Column

In a cave, where a stalagmite growing up has merged with a stalactite lengthening down, to form one continuous pillar of rock.

Convergence

Where two or more tectonic plates or other huge pieces of rock move together and push against each other, for example, producing subduction.

Core

The ball-shaped middle of the Earth, inside the mantle layer. It has two parts – the outer core, which can flow slowly, and the more solid inner core.

Crevasse

A deep crack or fracture in a glacier, where it bends and partly snaps as it goes around a corner or over an angle in the slope.

Crust

The outermost layer of Earth, consisting of solid rocks to a maximum of about 50 kilometres deep. There are two main kinds, oceanic and continental crust. The crust and the outermost mantle just beneath are separated into separate curved, jagged-edged sections called tectonic plates. See also Lithosphere.

Delta

The area of land or wetlands at the mouth (estuary) of a river, which usually widens to form a triangle or funnel shape as it enters the sea.

Divergence

Where two or more tectonic plates or other huge pieces of rock move apart and pull away from each other, for example, at a mid-oceanic ridge or rift valley.

Erosion

The breakdown and wearing away of rocks into smaller pieces by natural forces such as ice, rain, flowing water, frost, wind and heat. Erosion can also refer to the carrying or transport of these pieces to new places.

Fault

A large-scale crack, fracture or boundary between two or more tectonic plates or other huge pieces of rock. The visible path of the fault at the surface is called the fault line.

Geyser

Fossils

Remains of animals, plants and other once-living things that have been preserved in rocks and turned to stone.

Fumarole

A crack or gap at the Earth's surface through which fumes and vapours emerge, heated far below.

Geyser

An outpouring of water, spray and vapour ('steam') heated below the surface, which spurt from a hole or crack at the surface. Some geysers erupt often, others very rarely.

Glacier

A large ribbon or sheet of ice that flows slowly, usually downhill as a result of gravity.

Igneous rocks

Rocks that have been so hot and/or pressurized that they melted as magma or lava, and then cooled to become solid rock again.

Lava

Rock at the surface that is molten and can flow, due to the great temperature and pressure it was exposed to when it was magma, deep in the Earth. Lava usually emerges from cracks or gaps in volcanoes. It is sometimes also called lava after it has cooled and become solid.

Lithosphere

The crust plus the outermost part of the mantle underlying it. These two layers form the outer hard shell of the Earth and are broken into curved tectonic plates.

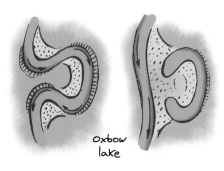

Oxbow lake

Magma

Rock beneath the surface that is molten and can flow, usually due to great temperature and pressure deep in the Earth. When it emerges at the surface it is called lava.

Mantle

The layer of the Earth below the crust and around the core, consisting mainly of rocks that are so hot and under such great pressure that they can flow slowly like thick milkshake.

Meanders

Bends or curves in a watercourse such as a river. They usually form where the slope is gentle and the river can change direction easily.

Metamorphic rocks

Rocks that have changed from their original form by being exposed to great heat and/or pressure, but not melted. Once cooled it became a different type of solid rock.

Moraine

Soil and bits of rock picked up, brought together and carried along by a glacier's movement.

Oxbow lake

A curved lake that was a meander or bend in a river that became cut off from the main river's course and is now isolated.

Sedimentary rocks

Rocks made from loose sediments that settle as layers and then become compressed or squeezed, and cemented by minerals and pressure, into solid rock.

Sediments

Particles from the erosion of rocks that are carried along by, for example, water currents, and then settle when the current speed slows. Sediment sizes vary from large boulders to tiny grains of sand, mud, silt and clay.

Seismic waves

Waves of energy, usually in the form of shaking or vibrations in various directions, that travel through the rocks, crust and other layers of the Earth.

Stalactites

Rock formations that hang downwards, usually long and pointed like icicles, suspended from the roof of a cave.

Stalagmites

Usually long and sharp-tipped rock formations that point upwards, rising from the floor of a cave.

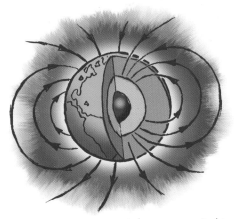

Earth's magnetic field

Subduction zone

Where two tectonic plates move together or converge, and one is pushed down under the edge of the other. Usually a thin oceanic plate is subducted beneath the edge of a thicker continental plate.

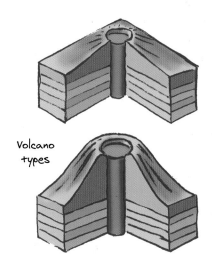

Volcano types

Tectonic plates

Curved slabs that form the hard, cracked outer 'shell' of the Earth, and which make up the lithosphere. Each plate consists of a portion of crust plus the outermost mantle just beneath it, and moves slowly in relation to its neighbouring plates. See Lithosphere.

Transform fault or zone

Where two or more tectonic plates or other huge pieces of rock move horizontally, sideways in relation to each other.

Tsunami

A large wave or series of waves caused by the movement of a huge amount of water, such as by an earthquake on the seafloor. Tsunamis are sometimes called 'tidal waves' but they have nothing directly to do with tides.

INDEX